Helping Children See Jesus

ISBN: 978-1-64104-024-2

God's Discipline
Old Testament Volume 13:
Numbers, Part 1

Author: Arlene S. Piepgrass
Illustrator: Vernon Henkel
Colorization: Courtesy of Good Life Ministries
Typesetting and Layout: Patricia Pope

© 2019 Bible Visuals International
PO Box 153, Akron, PA 17501-0153
Phone: (717) 859-1131
www.biblevisuals.org

All rights reserved. No part of this publication may be reproduced, stored in a retrieval system or transmitted in any form by any means, electronic, mechanical, photocopy, recording or otherwise, without the prior permission of the publisher, except as provided by USA copyright law.

RELATED ITEMS

To access related items (such as activities, memory verse posters and translated texts) please visit our web store at shop.biblevisuals.org and enter 2013 in the search box on the page.

FREE TEXT DOWNLOAD

To access a FREE printable copy of the teaching text (PDF format) in English or other available languages, enter S2013DL in the search box. Add the item to your cart, and use coupon code XTACSV17 at checkout. Once your order is processed you will receive an email with a link to the free download.

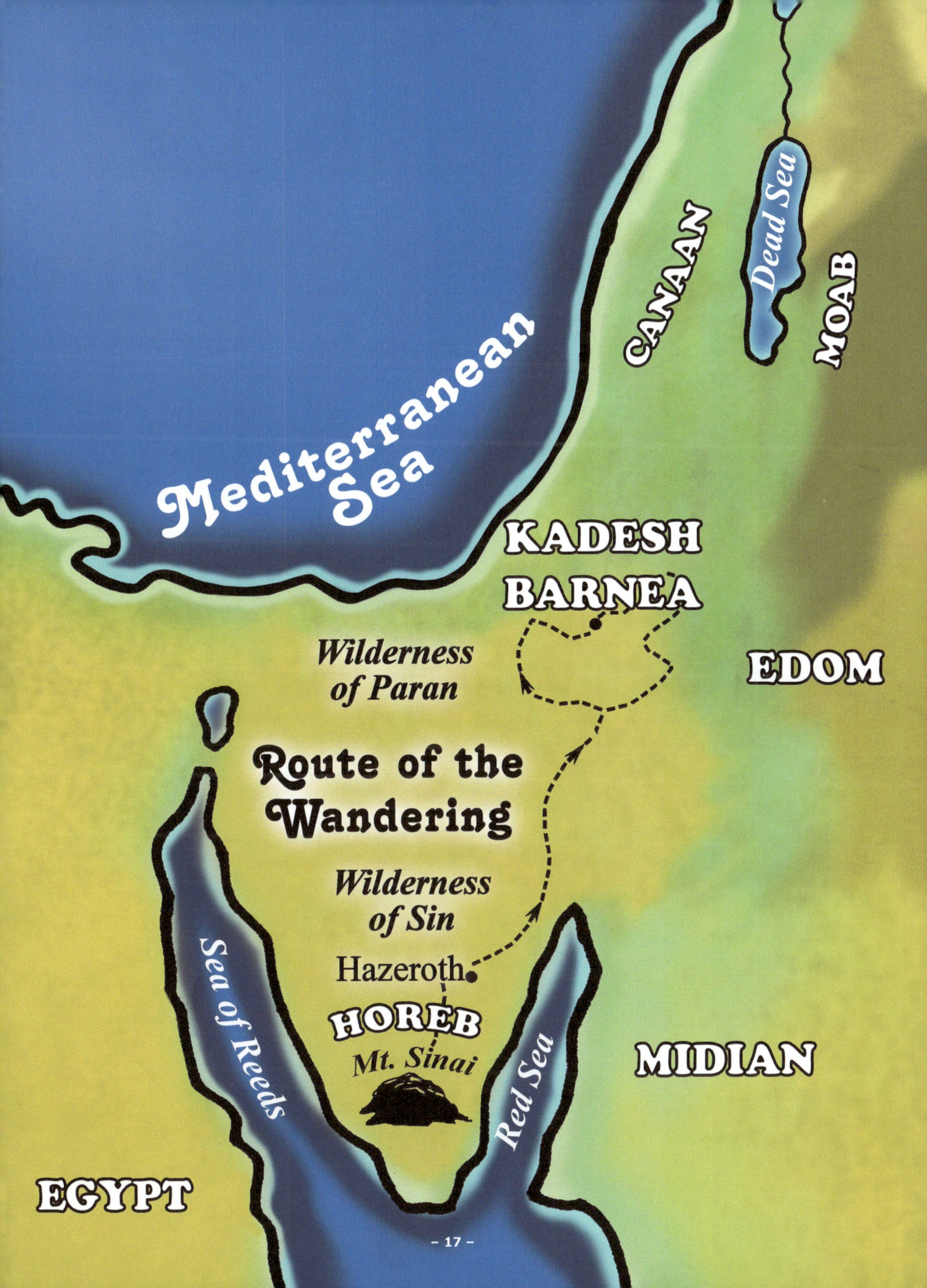

"And when the people complained, it displeased the LORD: and the LORD heard it; and His anger was kindled." Numbers 11:1a

Lesson 1
WONDERFUL EXPERIENCES—FORGOTTEN!

NOTE TO THE TEACHER

It is important for your students to understand and remember truths concerning what God did for His chosen people, the Israelites. This lesson, therefore, reviews the past. Create an atmosphere of thanksgiving to the Lord as you review. One year elapsed from the time the people of Israel left Egypt until they set up the tabernacle at Mount Sinai (Exodus 40:17). Leviticus covers a period of one month when God instructed Israel how to worship Him. So the events in Numbers begin thirteen months after the Israelites left Egypt.

Numbers continues the history of the Israelites' journey to Canaan. Their trek was extended to a total of 40 years because of their refusal to believe God and enter the land of Canaan. The book gets its title from the census taken at the beginning and at the end. It could also be called *The Book of Murmurings*. It records the repeated discontent and complaints of God's people. They murmured against God and their leaders, Moses and Aaron. This displeased God and He disciplined them severely.

Numbers is rich in incidents illustrating the Christian life, which is a pilgrimage in a world filled with danger and temptation. The lessons God taught the Israelites are helpful for our daily lives. (See 1 Corinthians 10:6.)

The first lesson will review the events of the previous year as recorded in Exodus and Leviticus. (See Volumes 6-12.) It is important for your students to understand the continuity of these books in the history of Israel. Only by repeated review will they retain what you teach.

Scripture to be studied: Psalms 78 and 99; review passages cited in lesson.

The *aim* of the lesson: To show that God wants His people to praise Him for all He has done (Psalm 107:2, 3, 8, 15).

What your students should *know*: Israel failed to remember God's goodness and consequently spent 38 years wandering in the wilderness.

What your students should *feel*: Thanksgiving and praise to God for His mercy and grace.

What your students should *do*: List specific instances of God's direction and blessings in their lives, beginning with their salvation. (Beware of forgetting as Israel did!)

Lesson outline for the teacher's and students' notebooks:

1. God's power (Exodus 12:12-51).
2. God's faithfulness (Psalm 78:12-29; Exodus 17:8-16).
3. God's laws (Exodus 20).
4. God's holiness (Psalm 99:3, 5).

The verse to be memorized:

And when the people complained, it displeased the LORD: and the LORD heard it; and His anger was kindled. (Numbers 11:1a)

THE LESSON

Did you ever listen to your parents as they talked about things that happened years ago? Often God told the people of Israel that they were to remember all He had done for them. When they faced hard times in their lives, they would then be reminded to trust Him again. (See Exodus 13:3; 32:13; Deuteronomy 5:15; 7:18; 8:2; 32:7.)

Today, let us pretend we are living in the camp of the Israelites over 3,000 years ago. Come to the tent where Nun, Joshua's father, is camping with his family. Listen as they talk together. Could it have been something like this?

1. GOD'S POWER
Exodus 12:12-51

"It has been 13 months since God led us out of Egypt," Nun recalled. "How wonderful it is to be free from the whips of those Egyptians! It is good to know that my children will not be slaves as I was."

Joshua exclaimed, "I shall never forget our last night in Egypt! Death wails filled the air. (Why? Let students answer.) I am surely thankful, Father, that you obeyed God by killing the lamb and putting its blood around our door."

"God had promised to protect our oldest sons from death if we did this," said Nun. "And He kept His promise. We must always celebrate the feast of Passover, remembering what God did for us that night." (See Exodus 12:12-51. Review feast of Passover celebration, Leviticus 23:4-5, Volume 12, lesson 1.)

Joshua's mother added, "I was really frightened when we came to the edge of the Red Sea. The Egyptian army came charging toward us and there was no way for us to escape. It seemed as if we all would surely be killed. But then God opened the sea right in front of us and we crossed over on a dry path!"

Show Illustration #1

She continued, "When our people were safe on the other side, God closed the water and all the Egyptian army was drowned. Immediately Miriam led us in singing praises to the Lord God for saving us. What miracles God did for us!" (See Exodus 14:13-31; 15:21, OT Volume 7, lesson 3.)

2. GOD'S FAITHFULNESS
Psalm 78:12-29; Exodus 17:8-16

Nun spoke sadly. "Since then, however, many of our people have been complaining. They seem to have forgotten what God has done for us. Instead of trusting Him, they grumble. They say they wish they had never left Egypt. How can they wish to be miserable slaves again?" (Teacher: review incidents of murmuring in OT Volume 8, lessons 1 and 2. Exodus 15:23-26; 16:2-3; 17:2-3.)

Show Illustration #2

Thinking of a later time, Joshua said, "I'll never forget the day I led our army against Amalek. The battle went back and forth for quite a while. Suddenly Amalek began to retreat. We totally defeated his army because Moses prayed for us. God was faithful in answering and giving us the victory!" (See Exodus 17:8-16, Volume 8, lesson 3.)

Joshua's family remembered. *But* most of the Israelites *forgot*. They forgot God's power. They forgot God's protection. They forgot God's faithfulness. They forgot God's promises. And God was displeased.

3. GOD'S LAWS
Exodus 20

Moses and Aaron, sitting by the tabernacle, were also remembering former days.

"Aaron," Moses began, "God has made clear His standards of conduct for us, His people. I pray we'll never forget His laws. God loves all the Israelites, but He is also just and He can't overlook disobedience. When we get to Canaan, our people will be tempted to worship idols for we'll see them everywhere. Idols are useless nothings. They have eyes, but they cannot see. They have ears, but they cannot hear. They cannot speak with their mouths (See Psalm 115:4-8; 135:8-18.) Our people will be tempted also to eat and dance as the heathen do when they worship their idols. There is always a great temptation for people to bow down to something they can see."

With a heavy heart Aaron remembered that sad day when he had made the golden calf (like the sacred bull of Egypt) for the people to worship. (See Exodus 32, OT Volume 9, lesson 2.)

Moses added, "We must continually remind our Israelite people that God has commanded us not to *make, worship,* or *serve* idols. Disobedience to these laws will bring punishment to our people."

Show Illustration #3

"Aaron," Moses continued, "I'll never forget those days on Mount Sinai when God talked to me from heaven. He who is holy wants us, His people, to be holy in our daily living." (See Exodus 19:6. Have students recall commandments of Exodus 20, OT Volume 9, lessons 1 and 2.)

It is easy to *say* we will obey all that God commands. How much harder it is to obey! We must continually pray that God will help us," said Moses.

Moses loved the Israelites. As God's appointed leader, he felt responsible for them. How he longed that they would obey God! He knew that only by doing so would God bless them.

But Israel forgot that God would discipline them for disobedience. They disobeyed and were punished.

4. GOD'S HOLINESS
Psalm 99:3, 5

Phinehas and his father, Eleazar, sitting near the tabernacle, also were talking about the past.

"Phinehas, do you remember why God commanded us to construct the tabernacle? Why did He tell us to set it up here in the middle of our camp?"

(Have students answer the question. God said, *"And let them make Me a sanctuary that I may dwell among them,"* Exodus 25:8.)

"We do not deserve God's presence in the middle of our camp," continued Eleazar. "God is holy. We are sinful. We deserve only His punishment. But God is also merciful. He does not give us what we deserve. Instead, He has provided a way for us to be forgiven. Do you remember what that way is?"

(Encourage student response. *Through the blood of a sacrifice.*)

"We must always thank Him and praise Him for this," said Eleazar.

As they sat talking, an Israelite neighbor walked by, leading a perfect lamb to the tabernacle door. Phinehas's uncle (Ithamar) was in the tabernacle helping his grandfather Aaron.

Show Illustration #4

Phinehas watched through the gate as his uncle took the lamb. The neighbor put his hand on the lamb's head. (Question students about this. It indicated that *the innocent lamb was taking the punishment of death which the worshiper deserved for his sins.* See OT Volume 11, lesson 1.)

Phinehas cringed as he saw the lamb being killed. Its blood was poured out. Because of the man's faith, he was forgiven by God for his sins.

"Father," Phinehas said quietly, "I am thankful I do not have to die for my sins. I am glad God accepts an animal sacrifice in my place."

"Never forget, Phinehas, that our sins cannot be forgiven without the shedding of blood," Eleazar admonished. (See Hebrews 9:22.)

"Father, tell me again about the other offerings which God told us to bring to the tabernacle."

(*Teacher:* Review briefly the five offerings as taught in Volume 11, lesson 1.)

> Burnt offering – consecration to God.
> Meal offering – thanksgiving to God.
> Peace offering – fellowship with God.
> Sin offering – forgiveness of sin.
> Trespass offering – cleansing for sin.

"The Most Holy Place is the most glorious part of the tabernacle, isn't it, Father?" asked Phinehas.

"Yes, my son. The presence of almighty God dwells there above the mercy seat. Perhaps one day you will be able to enter there as high priest," said Eleazar. (Explain the succession of the priesthood in the family of Aaron. Review the mercy seat from OT Volume 10, lesson 3.)

God said it was good for Israel to remember all He had done for them. *But* Israel forgot. The book of Numbers records their actions and attitudes which were rebellious against God. It records God's punishment for their forgetfulness and disobedience.

In our next lessons we'll learn how God disciplined His disobedient people. Today it is important for us to remember all He has done for us. (See Psalm 107:8-9, 15, 21, 31.)

Let's list some of His goodnesses and wonderful works which we should remember.

1. God is our *Creator*. He has given us our physical life (Genesis 1:27; Psalm 95:6; Isaiah 45:12).
2. God's Son, Jesus Christ, is our *Saviour*. He gives everlasting life to all who believe He died for their sins (Acts 16:31; John 3:16; Ephesians 2:11-13).
3. Christ arose from the dead (2 Timothy 2:8).
4. God supplies our needs (Philippians 4:19).
5. God hears and answers our prayers (Psalm 145:18-19; Matthew 21:22).

6. God cares for us (1 Peter 5:7; Psalm 55:22; Matthew 11:28).
7. God guides us in our lives (Psalm 32:8; James 1:5).
8. The Lord Jesus is preparing a home for us in heaven (John 14:2).

(Encourage each student to add to the list, including recent answers to prayers. Stimulate a spirit of praise and thanksgiving in the class as you recall together God's love and care.)

If we forget God's blessings, we complain and doubt and God must discipline us. Are you a praising Christian or a complaining Christian? Or, maybe you are not a Christian at all. If so, will you stay after class so I can show you how you, too, can enjoy all that God has done for you?

Lesson 2
DIVINE ORDER AND LEADERSHIP

Scripture to be studied: Numbers 1-10
The *aim* of the lesson: To show that God gives specific directions to His people.
  What your students should *know:* That God has a special task for each of His people.
  What your students should *feel:* A desire to learn what God wants them to do.
  What your students should *do:* Seek God's guidance every day.
Lesson outline for the teacher's and students' notebooks:
1. Arrangement of the camp (Numbers 1, 2).
2. Assignment of ministries (Numbers 1:47-54; chapters 3, 4, 8).
3. The guiding cloud and silver trumpets (Numbers 9:15-23; 10:1-36).
4. God leads us today (Psalm 119:105; John 16:13).

The verse to be memorized:

And when the people complained, it displeased the LORD: and the LORD heard it; and His anger was kindled. (Numbers 11:1a)

NOTE TO THE TEACHER

The words, "And the Lord spoke unto Moses," are repeated more than 80 times in the book of Numbers. God gave specific guidance to the people of Israel. He knew every Israelite and designated a place and service for each. God knows us too, and has a plan for each one (John 10:14, 27; 15:16). He desires to guide us day by day in each detail of our lives if we will let Him (Psalm 32:8). Remind your students frequently that the Israelites' experiences are examples and warnings for us. (See 1 Corinthians 10:11; Romans 15:4.)

We learn in these chapters that God does all things decently and in order. He wants His children to live disciplined lives under His direction. Be sure to read these ten chapters several times before teaching your students. As you teach the first section, continually use illustration #5.

THE LESSON

Did your family ever move to a different house or to a different town or village? What was your job in helping to move? (Allow response.) After you reached your new home, was it hard to find some of your things? (Let one or two students share an experience briefly.)

Think what it would be like for two million people with all their cattle and possessions to move at the same time! This is exactly what the Israelites were doing! (Teacher: compare the number of people with a city known to the students so they will get some idea of the size of the group.)

God led His people out of Egypt. He led them across the Red Sea and on to Mount Sinai. (Indicate on map.) They camped for a year at Mount Sinai. Here God gave them the ten commandments. He also gave them instructions for building the tabernacle.

On the very first day of the second year after leaving Egypt, the tabernacle was set up exactly as God had commanded. What a special day! The people watched as Moses directed the work. When it was completed a cloud covered the entire tabernacle. And the brightness of God's presence filled the Most Holy Place inside the tabernacle. (See Exodus 40:34.)

Not all the people could see the glorious brightness of God's presence. Why? *(Only the high priest was allowed to enter the Most Holy Place once a year.)* But they knew God was there, right in the middle of their camp, for He had promised to dwell among them.

1. ARRANGEMENT OF THE CAMP
Numbers 1, 2

The time came for the Israelites to move on from Mount Sinai. But first God had some important instructions to give them. He said:

1. "Moses, you are going to need an army." (Why do nations or tribes need armies? Apply to your situation and let students respond.) God knew the Israelites would meet enemies when they arrived in Canaan. They would have to fight battles.
   God continued, "Count all the young men who are 20 years of age or older. These are the ones who will go to war for you."
2. Next God showed the exact spot where each tribe was to pitch its tent in the camp.

Do you remember learning about Jacob when we studied Genesis? How many sons did Jacob have? *(12)* Each of his sons became the head of a tribe or family group. Jacob had died more than 200 years before the time of our present study. His sons had died, too. But the tribes of Israel still had the names of Jacob's sons.

Show Illustration #5

Each of the 12 tribes had a flag with their family emblem on it. (See Numbers 2:2; Genesis 49:1-28. Explain that the flags of countries often have emblems which tell something about the country. Just so the flag of each Israelite tribe told something about that family group.)

Moses listened carefully as God instructed him. "I want the leader of each tribe to raise his family flag on a pole. All the families in his tribe are to set up their tents behind his flag.

"Judah, Issachar, and Zebulun will place their flags on the east side of the tabernacle. Reuben, Simeon and Gad will raise their flags to the south of the tabernacle."

– 21 –

(*Teacher:* Indicate the location of each of the tribes. Emphasize the orderliness of God's arrangement. Point out that Ephraim and Manasseh were Joseph's sons–Jacob's grandsons. Levi was not included because that tribe served all the tribes religiously. (See Numbers 1:53; 2:33.) So Joseph's two sons were used to make the 12 (Numbers 1:32-35).

Think of this. God *knew* every person in the camp! And every family was assigned a special *place* to pitch its tent. There would never be confusion or arguing when they moved from placed to place. So, if we are in the place God puts us, we should avoid argument and misunderstanding by not trying to take someone else's place.

2. ASSIGNMENT OF MINISTRIES
Numbers 1:47-54; chapters 3,4,8

Whose tents haven't we mentioned? (*Those of Moses and Aaron*) The tents of Moses, Aaron, and the priests were at the gate of the tabernacle. Why do you think they camped in such a special spot? (Allow discussion.) They were the ones who took care of the tabernacle. What were some of the things that had to be done in the tabernacle. (*Offering sacrifices, lighting the candlestick; placing the incense on the golden alter; changing the loaves on the table of shewbread*)

Aaron had only two sons to help in all the work of the tabernacle –Eleazar (the father of Phineas) and Ithamar. Do you remember what happened to Aaron's other two sons, Nadab and Abihu? (*Teacher:* Review their disobedience recorded in Leviticus 10, OT Volume 11, lesson 2.)

3. God spoke to Moses again and said, "There is much work to do in taking care of the tabernacle. I want you to assign the tribe of Levi to help Aaron. Its young men shall not go to war. Instead, they will pitch their tents close to the tabernacle as do you, Aaron, and the priests." This was a special privilege for them.

Levi had three sons, Gershaon, Kohath, and Merari. Each of his sons had children and grandchildren. God commanded: "Gershon and his family will set up camp on the west side of the tabernacle. Kohath and his family on the south side; Merari and his family on the north side." (The gate was on the east and must not be blocked.)

When the camp moves, the tabernacle must also be moved," God explained. "It must *always* be in the center of your camp."

Moses listened carefully to God's instructions. Then he had a meeting with Gershon, Kohath, and Merari. He explained their special responsibilities.

"You and the young men in your families will have the privilege of moving the tabernacle when we journey. You will take it down, carry it, and set it up again. Kohath, your family will be in charge of carrying all the furniture of the Holy Place and the Most Holy Place. (Review furnishings.) You must always wait until Aaron and Eleazar cover these furnishings before you enter the tabernacle. If you go in before they are covered, you will die!"

Moses continued, "Aaron and Eleazar will place the furniture on poles and you will carry it on your shoulders. Be very careful not to touch any of the holy furniture. This is God's command."

"Gershon," Moses added," the men in your family will carry all the curtains and the skins which cover the tabernacle. You will also carry the altar and the laver."

Merari was waiting to hear what his family was assigned in this important task of moving the tabernacle. "Your responsibility will be to carry the frames of the tabernacle and the courtyard, the boards, posts, the sockets for the posts and the ropes," instructed Moses.

Show Illustration #6

The loads of Gershon and Merari were too heavy to carry on their shoulders. So the other tribes of Israel gave them wagons and oxen.

Each one had something to do and each one *knew* what his responsibility was. Each task was equally important. It had been assigned by God. Merari could have said, "Kohath, your work is more important than mine. I wish I could carry the furniture of the tabernacle instead of the boards and posts." But God wanted Merari to do his assigned duty cheerfully.

3. THE GUIDING CLOUD AND SILVER TRUMPETS
Numbers 9:15-23; 10:1-36

About seven weeks passed after the tabernacle was set up in the middle of the camp. Since Phinehas was a boy like boys today, he must have asked his father many questions.

"How long are we going to stay here, Father?"

"I don't know, my son," said Eleazar.

"Will Moses tell us when we're going to move?"

"No, God will tell us." answered Eleazar.

"How?" asked Phinehas.

"Do you see the cloud over the tabernacle, Phinehas?" asked Eleazar.

"Yes, it has been there ever since they put up the tabernacle. It is different from other clouds. It never breaks up. And I can see it in the dark as well as in daylight because it is so bright. At night, it looks like a cloud of fire."

Show Illustration #7

"That cloud is a sign of God's presence with us." explained Eleazar. "By that cloud, God will lead us. When it lifts and begins to move, we'll pack our things and move with it. We'll follow the cloud and keep traveling until it stops. When the cloud stops, we'll set up our camp again exactly as it is here."

Phinehas exclaimed, "It is wonderful that God will show us exactly were to go!"

"Yes, my son, this is a comfort. None of us has ever traveled through this wild country before. We wouldn't know the way. But with the cloud to guide us, we won't get lost." Eleazar assured his son.

"What'll happen if some of the men are away taking care of the animals?" asked Phinehas. "They may not see the cloud move."

"That's right, son," Eleazar answered. "So God told Moses to make two silver trumpets. When the cloud begins to move, your Uncle Ithamar and I will blow the trumpets. When the people hear the trumpets, they'll know it's time to pack their belongings and take down their tents. No one will be able to say he didn't know it's time to move. Everyone will be able to hear and see that God is leading us on. They aren't to make any plans of their own. They are simply to follow God."

4. GOD LEADS US TODAY
Psalm 119:105; John 16:13

Maybe you're thinking, *Why are we studying about the experiences of the Israelites?* God wrote down what happened to the people of Israel as examples for us. He wants us to learn helpful lessons from them.

Today we learn three lessons.

1. Just as God knew each Israelite, so He knows each one of us who belongs to Him. Those who believe on the Lord Jesus Christ become a part of God's family. (John 1:12). God knows each of His own by name! (John 10:3, 14.)
2. As God gave work to each Israelite, so He has a special task for you and for me. He wants us to be willing to serve Him where He tells us to serve. We are all to tell others about the Lord Jesus Christ, God's Son. (See Mark 16:15.) Some are told by God to be preachers or teachers. Some are needed to keep the church clean. Some are to earn money to help pay those who preach and teach. God has helpful duties for all. (See 1 Corinthians 12.) Are you asking God to show you how He wants you to serve Him? Then you should get the training you'll need to do His work well.
3. As God guided Israel, so He guides us today. We don't watch a cloud or listen for a trumpet. God has a better way to guide us.

Show Illustration #8

A. We have the *Word of God,* the Bible. By reading and studying it, we learn what God wants us to do, His Word is a "Light" for us to follow (Psalm 119:105).
B. When we become a part of God's family, His *Holy Spirit* lives within us. (See 1 Corinthians 3:16; John 14:16-17.) He will teach us and guide us if we allow Him to do so. (See John 14:26; 16:13.) He will help us make decisions. His guidance will always be agreement with the Bible.

Decide today to read God's Word every day. Instead of wanting your own way, ask the Holy Spirit to teach you and guide you in God's way. *Then follow Him!*

Lesson 3
THE ISRAELITES COMPLAIN

Scripture to be studied: Numbers 10:11-36; 11:1–12:16

The *aim* of the lesson: to show that God was displeased when Israel complained against His leadership.

What your students should *know*: That God punished those who murmured against Him.

What your students should *feel*: A fear of displeasing God by a complaining spirit.

What your students should *do*: Thank God for His blessings.

Lesson outline for the teacher's and student's notebooks.

1. Forward march (Numbers 10:11-36).
2. Complaining about God's direction (Numbers 11:1-3).
3. Complaining about God's provisions (Numbers 11:4-35).
4. Complaining against God's chosen leader (Numbers 12).

The verse to be memorized:

And when the people complained, it displeased the LORD: and the LORD heard it; and His anger was kindled. (Numbers 11:1a)

> **NOTE TO THE TEACHER**
>
> God blesses His people, but when it is needed, He also disciplines them. The incidents in our lesson today warn us against complaining. The Israelites grumbled about God's leadership. Their complaints were actually the rejection of the Lord's choices for them. Emphasize that one of the dangers of complaining is that it weakens our testimony for God.

THE LESSON

Do you ever complain about the food that has been prepared for you to eat? Do you ever grumble about what you are told to do? Do you complain about the work you are given to do? Why do you complain? (Let students respond.) Does grumbling make you happy? Does it make those around you happy?

When we grumble and complain, we are really rebelling against what others are asking us to do. God has told children to honor their parents (Ephesians 6:1-2). So when we complain against them, we are complaining against God. This is rebellion.

In our lesson today, we are going to learn what God did when the Israelites complained about His care and direction.

1. FORWARD MARCH
Numbers 10:11-36

Show Illustration #9

Eleazar and Ithamar blew loud and long on the silver trumpets. Everyone stopped what they were doing. All eyes turned towards the tabernacle. Shouts were heard everywhere.

"The cloud is lifting! We're moving! On to the land God has promised! Hurry, pack the tents! Herd the animals!" Everyone rushed about.

What do you suppose the mothers did to prepare for the journey? (Let students give ideas such as: *they packed cooking pots, got the small children ready, packed the clothes, etc.*)

What do you think the boys and girls had to do? *(Help with the animals, tie things in bundles suitable to carry, etc.)*

Aaron and his sons carefully covered the golden candlesticks, the table of shewbread, the altar of incense, and the ark in the Most Holy Place. Then the sons of Kohath lifted the furniture to their shoulders.

God told the exact order in which the tribes were to march. Each marched behind its own flag. There was no confusion. Three tribes went first. (Name the tribes if you feel it would be helpful to your students.) Then Gershon and Merari followed with the tabernacle on their wagons. Three more tribes marched behind their flags. The Kohathites followed with the furniture of the tabernacle. Behind them were the other six tribes. What a sight that must have been! More then two million people marching in order.

2. COMPLAINING ABOUT GOD'S DIRECTION
Numbers 11:1-3

All day long the people walked. The cloud of God led the way. The desert stretched out on every side. The people were not used to walking long distances. The Bible does not tell us what they grumbled about, but it does tell us that they complained. (See Numbers 11:1.) Could it have been like this?

"I am tired of walking. How far are we going before we can set up camp again?" grumbled one man.

Before long, others were complaining. "This is a terrible way to go. The rocks hurt my feet. Why did we ever leave Egypt? At least I knew where my home was back there."

"I agree," shouted several others.

The third day was even worse. When they settled down for the night, the complaints continued. "I cannot go on much longer," cried some of the mothers. "Where is Moses taking us anyway? I hate it out here."

Show Illustration #10

The leaders couldn't hear them. But God heard. Suddenly fire struck the outer edges of the camp! Tents began to burn. Possessions caught fire. God sent fire to punish them for their complaining. He was angry. He had taken good care of them. Now, instead of thanking Him, they were grumbling.

The people tried to put out the fire but couldn't. Some ran to Moses crying, "The camp is on fire! Help! Help! Pray for us, Moses! If the fire doesn't stop, our whole camp will be destroyed!"

Moses lifted his hands to God and prayed. God heard Moses and stopped the fire as suddenly as He had started it.

3. COMPLAINING ABOUT GOD'S PROVISIONS
Numbers 11:4-35

Did the people thank God for putting out the fire? We are not told. But as Moses walked through the camp he could hear the families talking in their tents. He heard a father complaining, "Manna, manna, manna. I am tired of eating manna every day. I want meat."

Someone else grumbled, If only we could have fish to eat!" "I miss the delicious melons more than anything else."

Complaining is as catching as a disease. It spread from one tent to another. The people were talking only of the food they longed for. No one was thanking God for all His loving care and provision. One cried, "I wish we had never left Egypt. There we could have all the food we wanted. We didn't have to eat manna there. Oh, I wish we could go back."

Did they forget how they had cried over their suffering while they were living in Egypt? Do *you* remember? (Let students review the miserable life they had in Egypt.) Did they forget that God was leading then to a land where they could have the best of everything?

Who was providing the manna for them? *(God).* So who were they complaining against? *(God.)* God heard them and He was angry. Moses heard them and he became so discouraged that he didn't want to be their leader anymore.

But God spoke to Moses. "These people have rejected ME, Moses. I am going to send them meat to eat–enough for a month. They will eat until they're sick of it."

"But where in this desert will You find enough meat for all these people?" Moses asked wearily. "Even if we kill all our animals we won't have enough meat for a month. All the fish in the sea wouldn't be enough to supply such a crowd!"

God asked, "Moses, do you think I don't have enough power to provide it?" Do you think God could supply that much meat? (Allow response. Give reasons for affirmative response, reviewing God's miraculous provisions before this.)

Show Illustration #11

The next day God sent a wind. Soon the air was filled with quail (birds). They flew so low that the people were able to catch them with their hands. There were birds in the camp. There were birds all around the camp in every direction.

Mothers, fathers, boys, and girls spent the whole day catching quail. They did not even stop to sleep that night. They continued to catch the birds all night and all the following day. Greedily they gathered all they could get for themselves. They grabbed more, more, more. Then they killed them and laid them out in the sun to dry.

Without thanking God for His miraculous supply of meat, they began to stuff themselves. No one said, "I am sorry I grumbled about the manna. I am sorry that I said I wanted to go back to Egypt. I am sorry I complained against God's leading." No! They were too busy eating and satisfying themselves.

Their selfish, ungrateful attitudes displeased God. Again, He became angry with them. This time He sent sickness and many i\of the people died. God gave them what they wanted, but sent sorrow and disappointment along with it (Psalm 106:15).

Surely now they would remember how much God was hurt by their complaining!

4. COMPLAINING AGAINST GOD'S CHOSEN LEADER
Numbers 12

The cloud lifted again and the people moved on (to Hazeroth). This time Miriam and Aaron began complaining. What do you remember about Miriam? (Help students to recall: *Moses' sister who watched over Moses in the bulrushes; she volunteered her mother to be nursemaid when the princess found him; she led the women in praising God when He led them safely through the Red Sea.*) Miriam was an important person in Israel.

What do you know about Aaron? (*He was Moses' older brother; he was the spokesman when Moses and Aaron went before Pharaoh; he led the people astray in worshiping the golden calf, yet he was appointed high priest by God; he alone could enter the Most Holy Place once a year.*) Next to Moses, Aaron was the most important man in Israel. Aaron and Miriam were leaders and should have been good examples for the Israelites to follow. They should have encouraged Moses in leading such a multitude of people.

Instead, they became jealous of Moses. Together they went to his tent and criticized him. Miriam said haughtily, "Moses, do you think you are the only one who can talk for God? God has spoken through us, too! Aaron is the high priest and I am a prophetess. We are leaders also!"

Who had chosen Moses to be the leader of the people? (*God*) So when Miriam and Aaron criticized Moses, they were really criticizing God. How dare they speak like that to the man God had chosen!

Before Moses could answer, God gave a command. "You three come to the tabernacle!" God came down in the cloud at the door of the tabernacle and spoke to Miriam and Aaron saying, "I have chosen Moses as My servant. I have spoken with him face to face–not in dreams or visions. He is faithful in carrying out My commands. You should be afraid to speak against him."

Show Illustration #12

Immediately, the Lord departed from the door of the tabernacle. As Aaron and Moses looked at Miriam, they were shocked. She was covered with leprosy! (Review the awfulness of this dreadful disease and the isolation it involved–Leviticus 13, Volume 11, lesson 3.)

"Oh, Moses!" cried Aaron. "We have sinned. Why did we speak against you? Why did we envy the place of leadership God has given you? Pray for Miriam. Ask God to forgive us."

Moses begged the Lord to heal Miriam.

God commanded, "Put Miriam outside the camp for seven days. After that she may come back healed.."

So the whole camp of Israel waited at Hazeroth until Miriam was healed. Everyone knew God had punished her for the sin of complaining. Again they were warned. Would they learn?

List in your notebooks some things you have learned in this lesson about complaining:

1. Complaining is really saying no to God's guidance in our lives.
2. God showed by His punishments how much He hates complaining.
3. God hears our complaints today and is displeased.
4. Complaining is catching and makes everyone unhappy.
5. Be careful not to criticize God's servants–preachers, teachers, leaders.
6. Thankfulness is the best cure for complaining.

Lesson 4
KADESH BARNEA–THE PLACE OF DECISION

Scripture to be studied: Numbers 13:1-14:45; Deuteronomy 1:19-46

The *aim* of the lesson: to show that God gives clear guidance to His people at the crossroads of life.

What your students should *know*: God expects His children to follow His directions and will chasten those who do not obey.

What you students should *feel*: Confidence that they can trust God in every situation.

What your students should *do*: Walk according to God's will even when it seems difficult to do so.

Lesson outline for the teacher's and student's notebooks:

1. The spies and their mission (Numbers 13:1-25; Deuteronomy 1:19-24; 8:7-10).
2. The spies and their reports (Numbers 13:26-33; Deuteronomy 1:33).
3. The decision of the people (Numbers 14:1-10).
4. The judgment of God (Numbers 14:11-45; Deuteronomy 1:34-46).

The verse to be memorized:

And when the people complained, it displeased the LORD: and the LORD heard it; and His anger was kindled. (Numbers 11:1a)

THE LESSON

Did you ever make a wrong decision and later say, "*If only* I had made a different choice? (Let several students give examples.) Why did you wish you had made a different decision? Wrong decisions can change our lives completely. Today we will learn about an important decision the Israelites made.

> **NOTE TO THE TEACHER**
>
> **Unbelief** is the word which sums up the Israelites' sad experience at Kadesh Barnea. Unbelief always shuts God out. Sending spies into the land was the equivalent of the Israelites saying they could not believe God. Nor could they trust Him to overcome obstacles.
>
> The people of Israel learned the bitter consequences of believing men rather than trusting God. God had caused the people of Canaan to fear the Israelites (Joshua 2:9-11). But this unbelieving generation of God's people never knew it. Instead, their own fears kept them from enjoying God's promises and provisions.
>
> How often do our fears and doubts govern our decisions, causing us to miss God's miraculous power in our behalf? Oh, that we would trust the Lord with all our hearts instead of leaning on our own feeble understanding or the understanding of others! Then we wouldn't miss God's best plans for our lives.

Have you ever gone on a long, long trip? Did you get tired? How did you feel when you were almost there? (Let students respond.)

After God had healed Miriam of leprosy, the cloud over the tabernacle lifted once again. The people packed their tents and continued their journey. On and on they went until they came to a place called Kadesh Barnea. This was right at the southern border of the land of Canaan. (Indicate on map.)

How thrilled Moses must have been! Two years had gone by since he had led these people out of Egypt and across the Red Sea. At last their journey was almost finished!

1. THE SPIES AND THEIR MISSION
Numbers 13:1-25; Deuteronomy 1:19-24;8:7-10

Moses announced, "We have arrived at the border of the land God promised to give us. He has told us there are springs and streams there, so we'll have plenty of water. It's a good land. There are fields of grain and fruit trees, so we'll have plenty to eat. We will not lack anything. Let us move in and take over! It's ours. God has given it to us!"

Show Illustration #13

But the leaders were afraid. Imagine that!

God had promised to go with them (Exodus 33:14). He promised to drive out their enemies (Exodus 33:2). He told them it was a good land (Exodus 33:3) He said He would bring them into the land (Exodus 6:8).

The Lord had overcome the greatest nation in the world–Egypt–to get them out of that land (Exodus 14:24-28; 15:1-13). Surely He would be able to defeat their enemies in Canaan (Numbers 10:35; Exodus 15:14-17). God had promised that the cloud by day and the pillar of fire by night would show them the way to go (Numbers 9:16-17).

But the people were afraid. Because of His love, God was patient with them.

"Moses," God commanded, "choose one leader from each tribe. Send these 12 men as spies into Canaan. Tell them to search out the land and see for themselves what it's like."

As the twelve spies prepared to leave, Moses challenged them: "Don't be afraid. Look over the land. See if there are many people or only a few. Find out if they are weak or strong. Learn whether they live in tents or in walled cities.

"Walk through the land and see if it is good for farming. Bring back some fruit with you. Be courageous!"

2. THE SPIES AND THEIR REPORT
Numbers 13:26-33; Deuteronomy 1:33

For 40 days the spies searched out the land. Then one day they trudged back to camp. People crowded around them.

Show Illustration #14

"Look at that huge bunch of grapes!" the boys exclaimed. Indeed the cluster was so big and heavy it took two men to carry it. Some were carrying other fruits– pomegranates and figs.

"What did you find?" the people demanded.

Everyone listened intently as the spies reported. "It is truly a wonderful land. Just as God said, there is plenty of food, milk and honey for everyone. You can see by these fruits that the land is very good for crops."

All the people nodded their heads in agreement. Imagine living in a place where they would have such a variety of good food–instead of just manna!

Ten of the spies had something more to say. "BUT, you should see the people! They are big and strong – much stronger than we are. They live in cities surrounded by high walls. We were really frightened!"

Two of the spies. Caleb and Joshua, spoke up. "Let us go and take over the land immediately. It is true that the people are strong. But God is stronger! It is true that the cities are great. But God is greater! We can conquer the people as easily as a person eats bread!"

The ten spies disagreed fiercely. "We could never conquer them. They are giants! We felt like grasshoppers beside them!"

Now the people had to make a decision. Only two spies (Joshua and Caleb) wanted to go into the land. Ten were against it. Whom should the people believe? (Let students discuss, giving reasons for their answers.)

What an important decision! Whatever they decided would affect the rest of their lives!

3. THE DECISION OF THE PEOPLE
Numbers 14:1-10

What should we do? Where shall we go?" cried the people.

"I wish we had died in Egypt," groaned some.

Others moaned, "If only God had let us die in the wilderness. The Lord has brought us here to be killed by those giants. Then they will take our wives and children as slaves."

All night long their weeping and wailing continued.

Then someone had an idea. "Let us choose a new leader in place of Moses. We'll go back to Egypt! At least we know what it is like there."

"Yes, yes!" others agreed. "That is a good idea."

"No, no!" shouted Caleb and Joshua above the noise and weeping. "Don't be afraid. Don't rebel against God. He will go before us. We won't have to fight the people, God will fight for us. Remember how He defeated the Egyptians? He will do the same again. It is a good land. God has given it to us. He is with us. Let's move in."

Do you think it was easy for Joshua and Caleb to stand against so many people? No, indeed. It is never easy to stand alone, even when we are right.

Show Illustration #15

Instead of listening to the two, the people shouted, "Stone them! Stone them! Get rid of them! We will not go up! We'll pick a new leader and go back!"

The people had made their decision. They would not believe God. They would not trust and obey Him. This was not only unbelief; it was mutiny!

4. THE JUDGEMENT OF GOD
Numbers 14:11-45; Deuteronomy 1:34-46

At that moment, the shining bright glory of the Lord appeared in the tabernacle. Everyone became terrified.

God said, "Moses, how long will these people despise Me? How long will they refuse to trust Me? I am going to kill all of them and make a new and greater nation with you as leader."

"O God, please don't do that," Moses pleaded. "The Egyptians will hear about it. They will say You didn't have the power to take Your people into Caanan. You are patient . . . . Show Your great mercy once more. Please forgive these sinful people."

"All right, Moses, I will pardon them as you asked. I won't destroy all the people. But they must suffer for their unbelief. They have refused to trust Me. They are stubborn and rebellious. Now they will be punished. Because they are afraid to enter the land I promised them, they will stay right here in the wilderness.

All the men who are now 20 years old and older will die in this wilderness. Then I will lead *their children* into Canaan. Their children will enjoy the blessings of living there."

God continued, "Caleb and Joshua believed I could take you all safely into the land. They believed I could defeat your enemies. After the rest of you die here in the wilderness, they will go into the land with your children."

Then, right in front of the people, God struck dead the ten spies who had brought the bad report.

It is truly "a fearful thing to fall into the hands of the living God" (Hebrews 10:31). We like to think only of God's love. We don't like to think about His anger. But God punishes sin. The price of unbelief is high. Remember, this is a warning for us. (See 1 Corinthians 10:6.)

When the people heard God's announcement, they began to weep and wail again. All night long they cried.

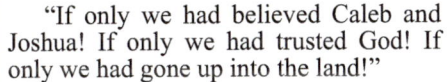

Show Illustration #16

"If only we had believed Caleb and Joshua! If only we had trusted God! If only we had gone up into the land!"

Early the next morning, the leaders came to Moses with a new idea. "We know we have sinned. We have changed our minds and decided to go into the land after all."

Moses quickly warned them against it. "It's too late. Don't even try it. The enemies you feared are still there. God will not go with you. You will be defeated."

But they were too stubborn to listen. They still hadn't learned that God means what He says. So they took their weapons, determined to enter the land without God's help.

What do you think happened? (Allow response.) Now they really were like grasshoppers. The people (Amorites) who lived there chased them out of the land, and they ran as if they were being chased by bees. Now the Israelites had no choice. Sadly they turned and wandered in the wilderness. What a sad, sad day! But it was their own fault.

Do you think anyone in Israel was happy that day? (Discuss.)

The Israelites deserved to be left alone–without God's help. Instead, He continued to lead them with the cloud. He continued to feed them with manna. He continued to provide water for them in the desert. God loved the Israelites. They were His special people. He punished them for their disobedience. But He did not leave them. He does not go back on His Word!

You must make decisions all through life. The most important is what you will do about the Lord Jesus Christ, God's Son. Have you decided to place all your trust in Him?

You also must decide whether you are going to live for God or for yourself. Name some ways you can live for God or for yourself. Name some ways you can live for God right now. *(Show love to others by being kind and helpful; obey those in authority over you; be honest: never lie or cheat; use language which is pleasing to God.)*

What are you going to do with your life? Are you wiling to serve God? What can you do right now to prepare to serve Him? *(Study the Bible; take advantage of every opportunity to learn skills; plan to get more training)* (Teacher: draw specific examples for your own group.)

These are decisions which you should make now. They will affect the rest of your life, just as the decisions that the Israelites made affected their lives.

How can you make the right decisions?

1. Read the Bible and know what God commands.
2. Pray and ask God to direct you.
3. Talk to Christians who have followed the Lord for a long time and listen to their advice.
4. Serve the Lord God right now–today.

www.ingramcontent.com/pod-product-compliance
Lightning Source LLC
Chambersburg PA
CBHW060804090426
42736CB00002B/149